Even if the mountains and hills disappear, my love for you will always remain.

Isaiah 54:10

Printed in the United States of America

ISBN: 978-1-968848-90-3- Paperback

ISBN: 978-1-968848-91-0- Hardcover

NBeirene Press

God's Love

Written by Nancy Owusu Adu

God's Love is deep

God's love is deeper than the ocean,

and reaches to the deepest part of me!

God's love is wide, and long, and deep. Ephesians 3:18

God's Love is Wide

God's love is wider than the sky

Love so wide, I can't wrap my arms around it!

God's love is wide, and long, and deep. Ephesians 3:18

God's Love is High

God's love is higher than the highest mountain.

It is so high I will never know it's full reach.

Your love is higher than the heavens! Psalm 108:4b

God's Love is Unconditional

No matter what I do, God's love for me will never change.

He cannot love me any more or less!

God showed us His love, even though we were bad people, Christ died for us. Romans 5:8

God's Love is Priceless

Love without a price tag is God's love for me. It is priceless!

Nothing can buy the love of God!

Your love is priceless. Psalm 36:7

God's love never fails

Although I may fail Him at times, His love for me remains.

It will never fail!

The love of God will never fail. Psalm 136:1

God's Love is Better

God's love is better than anything in life.

It is better than the best game or gift.

Nothing in this world can be compared to it!

I praise You always because your love is better than life.
Psalm 63:3

God's love is GREAT!

It has no beginning, and it has no end.

It cannot be measured or weighed on a scale.

He loves me more than I know!

Your love is great, it reaches to the heavens. Psalm 57:10

God's Love is Undeserving

Even though I try my best to stay out of trouble,

I still make mistakes.

But He loves me just the same!

He doesn't punish me like I deserve or pays me back according to my many wrongs. Psalm 103:10

God's Love Pursues me

It doesn't matter where I run,

God's love never gives up, it finds me every time!

I have loved you with an everlasting love. Jeremiah 31:3

God's Love is Expensive

Love so expensive, it cost God His only son....

Love so expensive I can never pay for it!

Greater love has no one than this, that someone should lay down his life for his friends. John 15:13 WEB

God's love is Forever

God's love will never end! It goes on and on and on.

It will last forever!

Give thanks to the Lord, because He is good and His love is forever. 1 Chronicles 16:34

About the Author

Nancy Owusu Adu is a Christian writer, a wife and mother of 3. With over 2 decades of experience teaching Sunday school, Nancy is passionate about bringing God's Word to life for both the young and young at heart. Among her published Children's books are titles such as God's Word Is, Jesus Gives Me, Who is Jesus to me, and many more. Outside of writing, Nancy enjoys reading, traveling, and connecting with family and friends.

Follow Nancy to stay connected

Instagram @ nancy.owusuak

Facebook @ Nancy Owusu Adu

www.ingramcontent.com/pod-product-compliance
Lightning Source LLC
Chambersburg PA
CBHW041446120626
46547CB00002B/372